POOR BEAST IN THE RAIN

BILLY ROCHE

Billy Roche was born in Wexford where he now lives with his wife Patty and their three daughters. His first novel, *Tumbling Down*, was published in 1986 by Wolfhound Press. He has written two stage plays, *A Handful of Stars* which won the John Whiting Award and the Plays and Players Award for the most promising playwright, and *Poor Beast in the Rain*, which won the Thames TV Bursary Award for the best play of the year. Both plays were first performed at the Bush Theatre, London. He is currently working on a television play called *Amphibians*, for BBC Scotland, and his next stage play has been commissioned by the Royal Court.

As an actor Billy has played Willie Diver in Brian Friel's *Aristocrats* at the Hampstead Theatre in 1988 and a small part in David Hare's film *Strapless*. His television work includes *The Bill*.

He has recently finished his second novel which is called *The Sound of a Lonely Note*.

As this book went to press, it was announced that *Poor Beast* had also won the George Devine Award.

by the same author

A Handful of Stars

BILLY ROCHE

POOR BEAST IN THE RAIN

NICK HERN BOOKS

A division of Walker Books Limited

A Nick Hern Book

Poor Beast in the Rain first published in 1990 as an original paperback by Nick Hern Books, a division of Walker Books Limited, 87 Vauxhall Walk, London SE11 5HJ

Poor Beast in the Rain copyright © 1990 by Billy Roche
Front cover design by Jim Bunker

Set in Baskerville 🎭 by Tek Art Ltd
Printed by Biddles Ltd, Guildford and King's Lynn

British Cataloguing in Publication Data
Roche, Billy
  Poor beast in the rain.
  I. Title
  822.914

ISBN 1-85459-053-7

Caution
All rights whatsoever in this play are strictly reserved.
Requests to reproduce the text in whole or in part should be addressed to the publisher. Application for performance in any medium or for translation into any language should be addressed to the author's sole agent, Curtis Brown Ltd, 162–168 Regent Street, London W1R 5TB.

Characters

EILEEN
GEORGIE
JOE
STEVEN
MOLLY
DANGER DOYLE

The play is set in Wexford, a small town in Ireland. It has a time span of one week-end, the week-end leading up to the All Ireland Final. Scene One takes place on Friday evening. Scenes Two and Three on Saturday Morning. Act Two, Scene One takes place on Sunday night.

Poor Beast in the Rain was first performed in London at the Bush Theatre, on 8 November 1989. The cast was as follows:

EILEEN	Catherine Cusack
DANGER	George Irving
GEORGIE	Gary Lydon
JOE	Des McAleer
MOLLY	Dearbhla Molloy
STEVEN	Denis Quilligan

Directed by Robin Lefevre
Designed by Andrew Wood
Lighting by Tina MacHugh

The play is set in an old fashioned betting shop. Stage left a counter runs into a wooden partition which is panelled here and there with frosted glass. A bench runs along the back wall of the shop. Stage right a few steps lead up into a little anteroom which has a couple of chairs and a table. There are three doors – one is the main front door and is situated stage left beside the partition. The second door is positioned behind the counter and seems to lead to an office. The third door is situated at the back of the anteroom, leading to a toilet and store room. There are two windows – one is a small curtained window behind the counter. The other is a big bay window in the anteroom. The counter is lined with all the usual stuff that can be found in a betting shop of this sort – pads and pencils and skewered dockets etc. Newspapers dot the walls. A speaker is mounted on the wall just above the bench.

ACT ONE

Scene One

Lights up on the betting shop. GEORGIE *is sitting on the wooden bench.* JOE *is sitting at the table, a spread-out newspaper in front of him.* EILEEN *is standing behind the counter. They are all listening to a race that is coming from a speaker on the wall.*

SPEAKER. And we're coming to the last furlong now and it's Dandy Boy, Elephant's Memory, Kissing Cousin, The Loafer and Napper Tandy all branching away from the rest of the field. And Elephant's Memory makes his move, cutting out on to the outside and Dandy Boy takes up the challenge and they're neck and neck now as The Loafer and Kissing Cousin battle it out behind for third place. But Elephant's Memory is inching forward and for my money it's going to be Elephant's Memory. It's got to be Elephant's Memory. Yes, winner alright. Elephant's Memory, Dandy Boy and The Loafer just shading it over Kissing Cousin for third with the favourite Napper Tandy well down the field.

EILEEN *writes in the winners on the result sheet behind the counter as* GEORGIE *palms a crinkled docket away.*

EILEEN. Hard luck Georgie.

GEORGIE. That's the story of my life.

EILEEN. Ah well, yeh nearly won.

GEORGIE. Yeah. But yeh know what they say about only nearly doin' somethin' though Eileen don't yeh?

EILEEN. No, what?

GEORGIE. Nearly never reaches.

EILEEN. Yeh got a good run for your money all the same.

GEORGIE. Yeah, I suppose I did.

SPEAKER. The starting price at Kempton. Elephant's Memory two-to-one. Dandy Boy eleven-to-two. The Loafer eight-to-one. Eighteen ran and the dual forecast was twenty seventy. Off five fifteen.

EILEEN *writes in the starting price on the result sheet and then she comes out from behind the counter to mark off the results on the sheet above the bench.*

GEORGIE. Hey Eileen, why don't yeh come up to Dublin with us tomorrow?

EILEEN. What?

GEORGIE. I say why don't yeh come up to the match with us? I'll get yeh a ticket.

EILEEN. Ah, I don't think so Georgie.

GEORGIE. Why not?

EILEEN. I'd look well now.

GEORGIE. But sure you won't be the only girl there yeh know. Some of the women out of the factory are comin' too. Anyway Eileen you'll be browned off hangin' around here because this place is goin' to be deserted over the weekend. Dogs and cats and all'll be gone boy.

EILEEN. Good. I'm lookin' forward to a bit of peace and quiet.

EILEEN *sighs as she works, sorting through a skewer of dockets.* GEORGIE *is over at the counter now.*

GEORGIE. Under pressure?

EILEEN. Yeah . . . I'm fed up of this place to tell yeh nothin' but the truth . . . Did yeh ever think of gettin' out of here Georgie?

GEORGIE. To go where like?

EILEEN. I don't know. Anywhere. I mean let's face it Georgie, we might as well be livin' in the back of beyond as livin' here.

GEORGIE. How do you mean?

EILEEN. Style-wise. Music-wise. Sure by the time somethin' reaches us here it's already got out of date everywhere else.

ACT ONE 3

GEORGIE. Aw I don't know about that now Eileen. I mean if a record comes out in England on a Monday say then you could nearly buy it downtown here the followin' weekend and that's not bad goin' for a little town like this.

EILEEN. Yeah well it's startin' to put years on me then. If it wasn't for me Daddy I'd be gone out of here long and ever ago . . .

SPEAKER. Newmarket weighed in. Weighed in at Newmarket.

EILEEN. Give us a shout if anyone is lookin' for me Georgie will yeh.

EILEEN *goes down to the office, a big ledger in her hand.* GEORGIE *watches her go.*

GEORGIE. Yeah right . . . She's a terrible nice girl Joe ain't she?

JOE. What?

GEORGIE. Eileen.

JOE. What about her?

GEORGIE. I say she's a fine girl.

JOE. Go away from me, will yeh. There's more mate on a butcher's apron. What did she mark down for third there?

GEORGIE. What? . . . The Loafer.

JOE. The Loafer. I thought so. I must remember that one. He should be worth a few bob the next time out. What price was he anyway?

GEORGIE (*sitting down on the bench, engrossed in a newspaper*). I don't know. Eight-to-one or somethin'. *Will Wexford regain the McCarty Cup?* Feckin' right we will. Jaysus look at the state of big Red O'Neill where he is. How would yeh like to be faced with the prospects of markin' that fella on Sunday now Joe? I'm goin' to tell yeh one thing but I don't think I'd sleep too well for the next couple of nights if it was me would you?

JOE. No.

GEORGIE. He's some big man though ain't he?

JOE. He is boy. There's no disputin' that alright.

STEVEN *enters.*

JOE. How's it goin' Steven?

STEVEN. Joe.

GEORGIE. Steven.

STEVEN. Georgie . . . Where's Eileen?

GEORGIE. She's down the back there Steven. Do you want me to give her a shout for yeh?

STEVEN. Ah no, it's alright. (*He is behind the counter now, examining the dockets and so on.*)

Eileen. Where did yeh put that big ledger eh?

EILEEN (*off*). I have it Daddy. Why, are yeh wantin' it?

STEVEN. No, it's alright. I'll do it after.

JOE. Well Steven, I suppose you're travellin' up to the match on Sunday are yeh?

STEVEN. Yeah.

JOE. Can a duck swim, says you.

GEORGIE. How are yeh gettin' up to it, Steven?

STEVEN. I'm goin' up on that auld bus out of Larkin's pub.

GEORGIE. The same as ourselves. Jaysus it's good deal though lads, ain't it? The bus, a meal and overnight accommodation for thirty-five quid. It's alright, ain't it?

JOE. We'll probably all end up sleepin' in the one bed. What do yeh think of our chances anyway, Steven?

STEVEN. Ah I don't know. When it gets to that level it could go either way.

JOE. That's a fact alright. There's a certain amount of luck involved in it all too ain't there?

STEVEN. Yeah – at that level, anyway.

JOE. Hey Steven, what do yeh think of all these women comin' along this year? Hah? I'm goin' to tell yeh one thing Steven, when you and me were runnin' the bus we had none of this auld codoligy did we? It was strictly a money on the counter, men only affair. These fellas haven't collected half the money nor nothin' yet I believe.

ACT ONE 5

STEVEN. Will we get there at all?

JOE. Now you said it Steven. Will we get there at all is right. Hey Georgie did I hear you sayin' that some of the women below in the factory are comin'?

GEORGIE. Yeah. Big Mag Delaney and all.

JOE. Big Mag is comin' is she? Oh be Jaysus little Mickey Morris'll be away with it so.

GEORGIE. How's that?

JOE. Sure big Mag is dyin' alive about Mickey. She came down to our section the other day there Steven lookin' for Mickey to open this great tin of beans for her. She was back again that afternoon with another tin for him to open . . .

JOE *winks. The others look at each other.*

Two tins of beans in the one day Georgie. I mean what is she, a friggin' cowboy or somethin'. Jaysus man John Wayne wouldn't go through two tins of beans in the one day . . . Did yeh tell Steven about the jersey yeh got Georgie? Big Red O'Neill tossed his jersey out into the crowd after the Leinster Final and the queer fella here was the one that caught it.

GEORGIE. Aw yeh should have seen me Steven. I was like Lowry Mar goin' up to catch it boy. I'm goin' to tell yeh one thing lads but it'd take the three of us to fill it. You could nearly rear a family in it man.

JOE. Give it to big Mag Delaney. She'd be well able to fill it.

GEORGIE. Hey there's only one fella wearin' that jersey on Sunday and that's me. And I standin' that way for the Boys of Wexford.

GEORGIE *stands to rigid attention and then suddenly bursts into a commentator's voice.*

And it's a glorious day here today in Croke Park. The sun is absolutely splitting the trees and shining down on the hardy men from Cork and the sturdy Boys of Wexford. And the ball is in and the game is on and Tommy James has the ball and he sends a grand lobbing ball across to Big Red O'Neill who goes ploughing through the backs like a big rhinoceros. And he takes his shot and it's a long

dropping ball and it's over the bar for a point for
Wexford. Cuilín amháin le Loch Garman agus tá sé
mahogany gaspipe. Tá sé bore the hole in the bucket . . .
I'm goin' to tell yeh one thing lads but if Wexford don't
win that match on Sunday I'll be fluthered drunk comin'
home on that bus. And I'll be even worse if they do win.

STEVEN *smiles a sad smile and makes to leave.*

STEVEN. Yeh might tell Eileen that I'm gone ahead home,
Georgie will yeh.

GEORGIE. Yeah, right Steven.

STEVEN. Oh and tell her too not to bother about the
evenin' paper. I already got one.

GEORGIE. OK.

JOE. Good luck Steven.

STEVEN. All the best.

STEVEN *leaves.*

GEORGIE. Ole King Cole . . . Hey Joe yeh have to hand it to
me though, I very nearly had him goin' that time didn't I?
For a minute there I thought sure he was goin' to laugh,
did you?

JOE. Huh, that'll be the day. Give us that paper there
Georgie will yeh?

GEORGIE *brings it to him.*

GEORGIE. And did yeh see the big coat and scarf and all on
him? I hope we don't get the weather he's expectin'. I
wouldn't like to see him in the middle of the winter would
you?

JOE. But sure that man is afraid of his life to let a bit of sun
in at him Georgie.

MOLLY *enters from the back room with a bucket and mop in her
hand.*

MOLLY. What won the last one Joe?

JOE. Elephant's Memory.

MOLLY *winces at the news.*

GEORGIE. Why, what did yeh back Molly?

ACT ONE 7

MOLLY. Napper Tandy.

GEORGIE. He was well down the field Molly. Mind you he ran a good race for yeh though. The other horses had to gang up on him. It took about fourteen of them to bate him . . . You're just after missin' Ole King Cole. He told us a couple of right jokes and everything here, didn't he Joe?

MOLLY. I'd say that.

JOE. Oh that reminds me Molly, did you hear anything about Danger Doyle being back in town?

MOLLY. Who was tellin' yeh this?

JOE. Ah some auld one that was in here today was sayin' that she thought sure she saw Danger Doyle walkin' along the Main Street early this mornin' with a suitcase in his hand.

MOLLY. I never heard nothin' about it then . . .

JOE. Well the news is out that he's back.

Silence.

GEORGIE (*whistles at the news*). Danger Doyle!

MOLLY. I doubt it . . . Mind you I wouldn't put it past him.

JOE. That was always one thing about Danger boy. You could never put anything past him. I remember one day meself and him robbed the nun's orchard and Danger cut the arse off himself on a big piece of glass as we were gettin' out over the wall. The blood was pumpin' out of him I swear. And do you know what he done boy? He got down off the wall and – with his pockets bulgin' with apples now – he went around and knocked on the convent door to see if they'd be able to give him a plaster or somethin' to . . .

EILEEN *enters and a hush falls on the little congregation.*

GEORGIE. Hey Eileen, your Da was here lookin' for yeh. He's gone ahead home.

EILEEN. Oh thanks, Georgie.

GEORGIE. And he told me to tell yeh that he already got the evenin' paper.

JOE. He's gone home to study the form for the match on

Sunday, Eileen. So you'd better keep your head down goin'
in the door because they'll probably be hurlin' balls flyin'
right, left and centre in there.

EILEEN. I'm well used to that Joe. (*She grabs a skewer of
dockets and goes back down to the office.*)

GEORGIE. Would yeh say she heard us?

JOE. I don't know. Sure what harm if she did. If Danger is
back in town she's goin' to have to get used to it anyway.

GEORGIE. Yeah, I suppose so.

MOLLY. Do yeh know somethin' boy, one of these days
you're goin' to get a right hand for yourself so yeh are.

GEORGIE. What do yeh mean?

MOLLY. Yeh think the sun, moon and stars shines out of
that one's face so yeh do. But like mother, like daughter is
what I always say. Of course yeh won't be told.

MOLLY *goes down into the office.*

Silence. JOE *chuckles.*

GEORGIE. What?

JOE. Ah I'm just thinkin' about Danger. Jaysus he was some
term boy I'm not coddin' yeh. 'Me Ma never even knew I
drank,' says he, until I went home sober one day.' Poor
auld Danger. We made fellas hop around here me and
him I don't mind tellin' yeh. Me and Danger. We were the
king pins in this town at the time so we were. Danger and
me. Yes, the king pins we were . . . Did I ever tell yeh
about all the times we used to break into this place?

GEORGIE. Yeah, yeh told me about that alright.

JOE. We used to break in through that big window there,
the pair of us, and we'd stamp a docket for maybe five to
three the next day or whenever and then when the race
was over we'd just write in the winner of it and that was
that. But of course the auld one that was workin' here at
the time eventually twigged it and they set a trap for us.
And do you want to know how she twigged it?

GEORGIE. The writin' was out in front of the stamp or
somethin' wasn't it?

JOE. Yeah. The writin' was out in front of the stamp instead of it being the other way around yeh see. It should have been behind it. She got suspicious when we came in to collect on a fairly big bet that she couldn't remember us placin'. She started examinin' the docket then and that more or less gave the game away on us. Mind you we got away with it for a long time. We were queer and lucky not to be sent up the river that time boy.

MOLLY *traipses through the anteroom again.*

I'm just tellin' this fella here about all the queer things meself and Danger got up to Molly. Butch Cassidy and the Sundance Kid we were like weren't we?

MOLLY. Abbott and Costello would be more feckin' like it.

She goes into the back room.

JOE. She was dyin' alive about Danger.

GEORGIE (*surprised*). Who, Molly!

JOE. Yeah. Oh Molly was a fine hoult in her day boy.

Pause.

GEORGIE. I'd say you'd like to see him again alright would yeh?

JOE. Yeah. And not blowin' me own trumpet or anything but I think I can safely say that he wouldn't mind seein' me again either.

GEORGIE. He sounds like a right chancer goin' around.

JOE. Yeah he was. Oh now they didn't call him Danger Doyle for nothin' Georgie.

JOE *returns to the newspaper.* GEORGIE *loses himself in thought.* EILEEN *returns and begins working through the skewer of dockets again.*

EILEEN. Well Georgie, are yeh goin' up to the dance tonight or what?

GEORGIE. What? Oh definitely. Sure it wouldn't be the same without me Eileen would it?

EILEEN. No.

GEORGIE (*going to her*). Are yeh goin' up to it yourself?

EILEEN. Natch. What band is playin' tonight anyway?

GEORGIE. Lugs McGuire and the boys. Did yeh ever hear him playin' Joe?

JOE. Who's that?

GEORGIE. Lugs McGuire. He's great on the auld guitar boy. Lovely chords and all.

JOE. I heard that alright.

GEORGIE. Someone was tellin' me that he's after composin' a song about Red O'Neill to the tune of Yellow River. It's supposed to be brilliant I believe.

JOE. But sure how could he get out of it. His Ma was a great musician too. She used to play the accordion with The Toreadors. The only woman in town with purple nipples.

GEORGIE *laughs*.

EILEEN. Do you know somethin', you two are disgustin' so ye are . . .

JOE. What!

EILEEN *chuckles*.

EILEEN. Hey by the way Georgie, did yeh notice anythin' different about me today?

GEORGIE. No. What is it, your hair or somethin'?

EILEEN *displays a locket around her neck*.

EILEEN. Nice ain't it?

GEORGIE (*examining it*). Yeah, it's neat alright.

EILEEN. I've just stuck a picture of me Mammy in there for the time being. Later on I'll get a proper one of her mounted in it.

GEORGIE. What is it, gold or somethin'?

EILEEN. Yeah. I hope so anyway.

GEORGIE. Who's it from, your Ma?

EILEEN. Yeah. It just arrived this mornin' out of the blue.

GEORGIE. What is it, your birthday or somethin'?

EILEEN (*nods*). Tomorrow . . . It's a nice lookin' yoke though ain't it?

ACT ONE 11

GEORGIE. Yeah. It's grand. Are yeh off Molly?

MOLLY *comes through the door, fastening her overcoat.*

MOLLY. Yeah.

GEORGIE. Are yeh goin' to come to the dance tonight?

MOLLY. I think my dancin' days are done boy.

GEORGIE. That's not what I heard then. Joe there was tellin' me that you were a right auld court in your heyday.

MOLLY. What the hell would he know about it? That fella'd shit himself now if he got a good court. I'll see yeh in the mornin' Eileen.

EILEEN. Yeah, see yeh Molly.

MOLLY *leaves.*

JOE. Thanks very much Georgie.

GEORGIE. She's some nettle ain't she?

JOE. She is boy! She's the contrariest woman I ever met and that's sayin' somethin' because I'm married to a one who can turn the milk sour with a glance first thing in the mornin', but I'm goin' to tell yeh one thing she's not a patch on her.

EILEEN. Oh I don't think I'd like to cross Molly somehow or other.

JOE. No, nor I either Eileen.

JOE *rises and goes out to the toilet. Pause.*

EILEEN. Hey Georgie, do yeh still hang around Byrne's Café these days?

GEORGIE. Yeah sometimes. How come I don't see you around there this weather?

EILEEN. But sure I only went in there when I was goin' out with Johnny Doran like yeh know.

GEORGIE. Oh that's right, Doraney was one of the king pins down there alright – on the machines and all. Well he thought he was anyway.

EILEEN *smiles fondly at* GEORGIE.

EILEEN. Is, 'One Way Love' still on the jukebox down there?

GEORGIE. Yeah Number 4B.

EILEEN. Aw is it? I love that do you?

GEORGIE. Yeah it's alright. Lugs McGuire and the boys plays that yeh know?

EILEEN. Do they?

GEORGIE. Yeah.

He sings.

> Must I always sing the same old song
> Every time I turn around you're gone
> Won't somebody tell me where do I belong . . .

EILEEN *singing softly while she works.*

> While you're up there and I'm sinkin' fast
> You must be livin' in a plastercast
> I don't want to spend my nights just thinkin' of
> One way love.

GEORGIE *stands there, drinking in the very sight of her and the lilt of her voice.*

EILEEN. There's only one thing I can't figure out about all of this though Georgie. The locket I mean . . . Accordin' to the guarantee it was bought down town in Carrington's.

GEORGIE. What's wrong with that?

EILEEN. Yeah but I mean what did she do, ring up Carrington's from London or what?

GEORGIE. Yeah, she probably did.

EILEEN. But sure she could have posted somethin' like this no bother. Anyway the card was written in her own handwritin' . . . I'm just wonderin' now if maybe me Mammy's in town, that maybe she came home for a bit of a holiday or somethin'.

GEORGIE. Naw. You would have heard somethin' Eileen.

EILEEN *sighs and touches the locket.*

EILEEN. I'm dyin' to see her again though Georgie. I know I'm always goin' on about her and all but . . . Ah I don't know. Ten years is a long time and a picture in a locket is not the same as the real thing, is it? It'll be her anniversary on Monday, yeh know?

GEORGIE. What do yeh mean?

EILEEN. It was the day after the All Ireland Final that she went away, sure. Yeh know I haven't got a clue what Danger Doyle looks like but I keep imaginin' that he's real handsome – like someone you'd see in the pictures. Jack Nicholson or someone.

GEORGIE. Jack Nicholson! He's not good lookin'.

EILEEN. Ah he is Georgie. I think he is anyway. I think he's deadly lookin'. Why who would you call good lookin' now?

GEORGIE. I don't know. Big Red O'Neill or someone.

EILEEN. Ah go away out of that Georgie, a big farmer goin' around.

GEORGIE. I'm tellin' yeh Eileen, come Sunday every woman in the town'll be after him because he's the man who's goin' to take us there. That's who you should be puttin' in your locket, girl . . . Hey Joe, show Eileen that picture in the paper of Big Red.

JOE (*returning*). What?

GEORGIE. I say I'm just tellin' Eileen here that Big Red is the man who's goin' to take us there on Sunday.

JOE. He'd better Georgie because I'm goin' to put a fiver on them now. If he don't score three or four goals this Sunday his photograph is comin' down off of my mantelpiece and that's all's about it.

GEORGIE. That's what I like about Joe. He's patriotic to the core.

JOE. When there's money at stake, Georgie, my allegiance goes out the window. Are yeh wantin' to come in on it with me? (JOE *is writing out a docket*.)

GEORGIE. What? Yeah, alright . . . Hey Eileen I'll get yeh that record for your birthday – 'One Way Love', I mean.

EILEEN. No yeh won't. You can't afford to be spendin' money on me at all. It's alright Georgie, I'll get it meself durin' the week.

GEORGIE. No I'll get it for yeh. Anyway who said anythin'

about spendin' money. By this time tomorrow number 4B will be gone missin' from Byrne's jukebox.

JOE (*handing* GEORGIE *a docket and money*). Here boy, go make yourself useful.

EILEEN. Georgie Whelan, don't you dare do that. I don't want you gettin' in any trouble over me at all. Anyway the centre is always gone out of those jukebox records. Georgie do yeh hear me talkin' to yeh.

GEORGIE. Stop fussin' woman will yeh.

JOE. Come on Georgie will yeh, 'til I go and get the tay.

GEORGIE, *a broad grin on his face, hands* EILEEN *the docket.*

EILEEN (*stamping the docket*). You're not to, Georgie.

GEORGIE *chuckles and examines the money in his hand.*

GEORGIE. Hey Joe, what's goin' on here?

JOE (*buttoning his coat up*). What? Yeah! You owe me a pound from the other day.

Lights down.

Scene Two

Lights up on the betting shop. EILEEN *is behind the counter.* MOLLY *is singing 'Dream Lover', as she works, dusting and polishing etc.*

MOLLY. Well Eileen, was the dance any use last night after?

EILEEN. Yeah it was alright. I enjoyed it anyway.

MOLLY. Yeh don't sound too enthusiastic about it then? The talent must have been scarce on the ground or somethin' was it?

EILEEN. Ah the usual yeh know. Sure all the nice fellas are gone Molly.

MOLLY. Hey Eileen, forget about the nice fellas. It's the bold boys yeh'd want to get your hands on. They're more fun. It's someone with a bit of jiss in him yeh'd want.

ACT ONE 15

Anyway what's all this sudden interest in nice fellas? I thought you were supposed to be partial to the wild boys.

EILEEN. What do yeh mean?

MOLLY. But sure weren't you all great with your man who ran away with the carnival last year. Whatshisname . . . Johnny Doran?

EILEEN. Oh yeah. Johnny was a bit wild alright.

MOLLY. A bit wild is puttin' it mildly I think Eileen. Didn't someone have a baby for him recently there?

EILEEN. Yeah.

MOLLY. That's not his picture you've got in that locket that you keep playin' with is it?

EILEEN. No. That's me Mammy.

MOLLY. Mmn . . . I'd say you were fairly fond of him though Eileen were yeh?

EILEEN *shrugs*.

What?

EILEEN. I don't know. He was different yeh know. He was a right bit of laugh and he was . . . Ah I don't know. He was just sort of different, that's all.

MOLLY. I know what yeh mean hon. I used to know a fella like that one time meself. Jaysus he's was a real hardcase too goin' around – swaggerin' about the place, puttin' on the agony as they say.

EILEEN. What happened to him?

MOLLY. What . . .? He went away . . . So this was a present from your Ma was it?

MOLLY *touches the locket*.

EILEEN. Yeah.

MOLLY. Yeh must have a roomful of stuff from her by now have yeh?

EILEEN. I surely have. You can hardly get into my bedroom with all the things me Mammy is after sendin' me over the years – toys and books and dolls and all. And as for jewellery! I've a music box that's absolutely overflowin' with jewellery. I mean I literally can't fit anythin' else into it.

MOLLY. Yeah well my advice to you is to take all yeh can get from her while it's goin' because it's not goin' to last yeh know.

EILEEN. What do yeh mean?

MOLLY. If I know your Ma as soon as you begin to blossom she won't want to know yeh. She don't like anyone tryin' to muscle in on her territory yeh see . . . I remember her down in Byrne's Café years ago and she swishin' across to the jukebox, a great skin-tight jeans on her and all. I'll give her one thing, when she walked across a room heads turned. She was a little older than me and I remember thinkin' at the time that as soon as she moved on I'd take her place.

EILEEN. And did yeh?

MOLLY. She never moved on. She hung back to claim the heart of the latest little tearaway in town. She did that for years.

EILEEN. What about me Daddy?

MOLLY. She met him at a dance somewhere. None of us could believe it when it was announced that they were gettin' married. A few weeks before she was ridin' around on the back of somebody else's motor bike. If she was here today she'd probably be dancin' cheek to cheek with Johnny Doran or someone. Huh, speakin' of wild fellas.

GEORGIE *has just entered, dressed up in his good suit and carrying an overnight bag.*

Well Georgie, any joy at the dance last night?

GEORGIE. Naw.

MOLLY. Ah go away out of that boy, you're a dead loss so yeh are. Eileen is only after tellin' me that there was lashin's of talent there last night.

GEORGIE. Yeah well I didn't see a whole lot of it then.

EILEEN. Thanks very much Georgie.

GEORGIE. What?

MOLLY. Get out of it Georgie Whelan, yeh wouldn't get off

in Hyde Park with a fiver in your hand.

GEORGIE. I'm goin' to tell yeh one thing but some of them there last night would nearly want to pay me a fiver just to dance with them.

MOLLY. God blast yeh anyway, anyone'd think he was Robert Redford or someone goin' around. Hey I like the suit Eileen, do you? Ain't he all out in his coughdrops now? Me Da got married in a suit just like that yeh know?

GEORGIE. Did he? Were yeh at the weddin' yourself?

MOLLY. Get out of it yeh little get yeh before I break your feckin' face for yeh.

GEORGIE *laughs.*

EILEEN. It won't be long now, Georgie.

GEORGIE. No. The bus should be pullin' in any minute now and then we'll hit the high road.

MOLLY. Have yeh no fancy hat to wear?

GEORGIE. I don't need a fancy hat Molly. I have this. (*He pulls out a massive jersey from his bag and holds it up to the light.*)

EILEEN. Where did yeh get that Georgie?

GEORGIE. Believe it or not this once belonged to the great Red O'Neill. He whipped it off of him after the Leinster Final and he tossed it out into the crowd and yours truly was the one who caught it.

MOLLY. By Jaysus you'll be a fine fella when that fits yeh.

GEORGIE. I will won't I? The size of it! I'll be wearin' this jersey tomorrow at the match. What am I talkin' about, I'll probably be wearin' this in the bed in that hotel tonight. That's provided that I get to bed at all of course.

STEVEN *enters.*

Well Steven, what do yeh think of that then?

STEVEN. What?

GEORGIE. This is the jersey I was tellin' yeh about. Red O'Neill's. I'll be a fine fella when that fits me won't I?

STEVEN. Yeah . . . Eileen, where did yeh put that big flask eh?

EILEEN. I don't know Daddy. Is it not in the cupboard in the hall?

STEVEN. No, I already looked there.

EILEEN. Well try up on the shelf in the kitchen behind all the jars and all. I think that's where I put it alright.

MOLLY. What do yeh think of the locket she got Steven? It's a nice lookin' yoke ain't it?

STEVEN. Yeah.

MOLLY. Ain't it well for her? So are yeh all set for tomorrow Steven?

STEVEN. Yeah. All set. Just waitin' on the auld bus to arrive now and we'll be off.

GEORGIE (*putting the jersey away*). Any sign of it yet Steven?

STEVEN. No. No sign of it yet.

MOLLY. Are we goin' to win Steven?

STEVEN. I don't know that. To tell yeh the truth so long as it's a good, hard and clean game I'm not that pushed which way it goes.

MOLLY. Mmn . . . I'd prefer to win it meself. You can keep your hard and clean game so long as we win it. Maybe that sounds a bit primitive but . . .

STEVEN. Ah no. Everyone has their own way of lookin' at it. So long as you row in behind your team that's all that counts.

MOLLY. Is it?

STEVEN. Yeah. Get behind your team. Get behind your town.

MOLLY. Do you hear that Georgie? You're to get behind your town. I bet yeh Steven has a fancy hat to wear tomorrow have yeh Steven?

STEVEN. What?

MOLLY. I say I bet you have a fancy hat to . . . Ah don't tell me you have n'er a hat either. Jaysus what kind of fellas are ye at all eh?

STEVEN *goes across and lays a little parcel of money on the counter for* EILEEN — *some silver wrapped up in a few pound notes.*

STEVEN. There's a few bob for your birthday hon.

EILEEN. Oh thanks very much Daddy.

STEVEN *smiles.*

MOLLY. He didn't forget yeh, all the same Eileen. Hey Steven, what's all this I hear about a crowd of women goin' along to the match this year? I hope there'll be no hanky-panky goin' on up there now?

STEVEN. I'll see yeh tomorrow night, Eileen.

EILEEN. Right Daddy. Enjoy yourself.

MOLLY. Don't do anythin' I wouldn't do now Steven.

STEVEN *ill at ease, leaves.* EILEEN *and* MOLLY *look at each other.* MOLLY *goes out into the back room.*

GEORGIE (*oblivious to the whole thing*). Oh that reminds me Eileen, I have somethin' for you too. (*He takes the record from his bag and hands it to her.*)

EILEEN. What? I don't believe it. 'One Way Love'. Jesus. Thanks Georgie. I'm goin' to tell yeh one thing but I dearly hope that the cops won't be after me for this.

GEORGIE. No you'll be alright Eileen. I was wearin' kid gloves at the time. The centre is gone out of it but that's no bother to fix. I'm nearly certain I have a centre piece at home anyway. It just sort of clips into it like, yeh know. It's alright though ain't it?

EILEEN. It's grand. I'll play this to death all day tomorrow now.

GEORGIE. Yeah I know. You'll probably drive half the street demented. It serves 'em right anyway for not goin' up to the match.

EILEEN. 4B missin' from Byrne's jukebox.

GEORGIE. What? Yeah. There'll be big headlines in next week's paper. 4B missin' from Byrne's jukebox. A special version of 'One Way Love' which was imported direct from the UK.

EILEEN. Ah no Georgie, me heart wouldn't be able for it.

GEORGIE. I'm goin' to tell yeh one thing if they call to my house I'll say . . . (*He gives a little whistle and points to her.*)

EILEEN. I'll tell them you gave it to me.

GEORGIE. I'll deny all knowledge. I'll say fingerprint me. Don't worry about it Eileen, I'll come and visit yeh when you're inside, bring yeh banana sandwiches and all.

EILEEN *laughs, her whole face radiating. She reaches out and kisses* GEORGIE *on the cheek.*

EILEEN. Thanks very much Georgie. I'd better put it away before somebody sees it.

She puts the record under the counter. GEORGIE *watches her, spellbound.* JOE *enters.*

JOE. Do yeh know what boy but I'm queer and glad that I've nothin' to do with the organisin' of that big bus.

EILEEN. Why, what happened Joe?

JOE. Little Mickey Morris is fast asleep on the counter already and two other lads are threatenin' to box over who's goin' to sit in the front seat.

JOE *waves it all away.* MOLLY *enters.*

MOLLY. Look at him all done up to go to a feckin' auld match.

JOE. The All Ireland Final Molly.

MOLLY. Huh.

GEORGIE. Who are you goin' to be cheerin' for tomorrow Molly?

MOLLY. None of 'em. I hope the two of them lose. A waste of bloody money so it is. And I'm only after washin' that floor so none of you need go traipsin' across it at all.

MOLLY *goes into the office.*

JOE. I heard that song that young Lugs McGuire made up about Red O'Neill after.

GEORGIE. Did yeh? Why is he over in Larkin's?

JOE. Yeah, he's over there with the auld guitar and all. Jaysus it's good ain't it?

GEORGIE. Aw it's very well put together alright. The boys played it last night at the dance.

JOE (*sings*).
>Who's the one who can take us there
>To Croke Park or anywhere
>Who's the man that they all fear
>Red O'Neill is
>Red O'Neill is

GEORGIE *joins in.*
>Red O'Neill is
>Red O'Neill is
>Da da da da da da
>Red O'Neill is
>Red O'Neill is
>Da da da da da da . . .

They run out of words.

JOE. I'm goin' to tell yeh one thing boy but that could be a hit – in this country anyway.

Pause.

GEORGIE. Where's your bag Joe?

JOE. It's over in Larkin's pub.

GEORGIE. Have yeh much stuff?

JOE. No.

Silence.

EILEEN. Hey Georgie, did you hear anythin' about Danger Doyle being back in town?

GEORGIE. What? Oh yeah, I heard somethin' about that alright.

EILEEN. So it looks like I was wrong about me Mammy comin' home then?

GEORGIE. Yeah . . . it looks like it.

Pause.

EILEEN. And have yeh any idea where he's stayin'?

GEORGIE. No. Do you know where he's stayin' Joe?

JOE. I heard he was stoppin' down in the County Hotel.

EILEEN *nods and nervously touching her locket she bends her head to her work.*

Lights down.

Scene Three

Lights up on the betting shop. GEORGIE *is sitting in the alcove of the bay window while* JOE *paces up and down the floor irritably.*

JOE. Lord Jaysus ain't this awful, ain't it? We should have left this street three quarters of an hour ago nearly. I don't know . . . This is ridiculous now so it is.

EILEEN *comes out from behind the partition.*

Well Eileen, what did he say?

EILEEN. He said the bus left the garage about twenty minutes ago.

JOE. Twenty minutes ago! By Jaysus he must be comin' via the friggin' Alps then. Did yeh tell him I was on the verge of losin' the head here?

EILEEN. Yeah, I told him that.

JOE. What did he say?

EILEEN. He said, 'So what else is new?'

JOE (*amused*). Did he? (*He chuckles.*) . . . Well I'll give them about another five or ten minutes and then the deal is off.

EILEEN. Georgie keep an eye on the place for me there will yeh? I'm just wantin' to see me Daddy for a minute.

GEORGIE (*in a trance*). Yeah right.

JOE. Don't be too long Eileen because we're goin' the minute that bus arrives.

EILEEN. I won't be long. Sure I'll see the bus from the pub anyway. (*She goes.*)

JOE. I don't know. I'm not coddin' yeh boy they wouldn't be able to run a whorehouse, most of them. Yes, they

ACT ONE 23

wouldn't run a whorehouse.

GEORGIE (*out of the blue*). It must be great to have your own girl Joe, is it?

JOE. What?

GEORGIE. Yeh know someone to dance with and all. Someone to take home. Maybe bring her to the pictures now and again.

JOE. But sure there's lashin's of girls out there to dance with.

GEORGIE. Yeah I know but it's not the same as havin' your own girl though is it? I'd like to have me own girl now.

JOE. Is that what you were thinkin' about all this time?

GEORGIE. What?

JOE. I was wonderin' why you were so quiet.

GEORGIE. I wasn't quiet.

MOLLY *enters*.

JOE. You were like a little mouse there so yeh were.

MOLLY. What's wrong with him now?

JOE. Oh he's thinkin' about Eileen again.

GEORGIE. I never even mentioned Eileen.

MOLLY. Do yeh know somethin' boy, he absolutely worships the ground that that one walks on, don't he? But you'll get a right kick in the arse one of these days boy when yeh wake up to find that she's not all that she's made out to be.

GEORGIE. Will you go away out of that Molly, nobody's all they're made out to be accordin' to you.

MOLLY. Yeah and her even more so . . . You can laugh all yeh like boy but you'll rue the day that yeh ever laid eyes on that one yet, so yeh will, you mark my words.

MOLLY *picks up the mop and bucket and goes down into the back room.*

GEORGIE. All I said was that I wouldn't mind havin' me own girl.

JOE. You're lookin' for someone special though Georgie.

GEORGIE. And what's wrong with that? Look I just want to make sure that I don't end up with someone who's goin' to turn into Molly the minute I turn me back on her.

JOE. They're all in danger of turnin' into Molly son. The same as you're in danger of turnin' into me.

GEORGIE. What?

JOE. Yeah. Strange as it may seem I was once just like you yeh know – a little Jack the Shillin' goin' around who didn't know his arse from his elbow. And look at me now! It's all before yeh boy . . . It's all before yeh.

Pause.

GEORGIE. Don't mind me askin' yeh Joe, but what's Molly always hintin' at about Eileen?

JOE. What do yeh mean?

GEORGIE. Every time she catches me lookin' at Eileen or talkin' about her she tries to make out that there's somethin' goin' on that I don't know about.

JOE. Ah yeh know Molly. She's probably tryin' to make out that Eileen is the same as her Ma at the back of it – a bit of a skeet goin' around.

GEORGIE. How can she say that Joe?

JOE. Well there was a bit of a rumour goin' around last year alright that when Eileen was goin' out with your man who ran away with the circus or the carnival or whatever . . .

GEORGIE. Johnny Doran?

JOE. Yeah, young Doran.

GEORGIE. What about him?

JOE. Ah there was a bit of a rumour goin' around that he managed to get Eileen into the bed one time while Ole King Cole was away at a match somewhere.

GEORGIE. Who told yeh that?

JOE. No one in particular told me Georgie. It was just a rumour.

GEORGIE. I never heard nothin' about it then.

JOE. Yeah well I suppose nobody had the heart to tell yeh

seein' how yeh practically genuflect every time Eileen's name is mentioned ... Anyway it was just a rumour.

GEORGIE *is devastated.* JOE *continues to pace up and down.*

Aw this is disgraceful. Look at the time it is. Well I'm goin' to give them about five more minutes and then I'm goin' over to Larkin's to demand me money back. If they can't keep up their end of the bargain then I don't see why I should be expected to keep mine ...

DANGER DOYLE *is standing in the doorway.*

DANGER. Are you still givin' out boy?

JOE. What? Who's that? Danger Doyle, me auld segotia, what way are yeh at all? Come in ...

DANGER. Come in, he says. Anyone'd think that he owned the place or somethin'.

JOE. I'm goin' to tell yeh one thing Danger but I must have a share in it at this stage. Put it there me auld stock, long time no see.

They shake hands.

DANGER. How are yeh keepin' Joe?

JOE. Alright. Jaysus Danger, it's a queer long time since I saw you last boy.

DANGER. It's a long time alright Joe – nine, nearly ten years now sure.

JOE. What? Yeah it would be ... I don't mind tellin' yeh but yeh caused a fair bit of a stir around here too yeh fucker yeh.

DANGER. What before I left yeh mean?

JOE. Before and after. For a long time after.

DANGER. Yeah, I can imagine. I suppose I was the talk of the town was I?

JOE. Danger, your name echoed from every dance hall in the land boy ... So how is herself?

DANGER. Grand. Right form.

JOE. She didn't come over with yeh, no?

DANGER. No.

JOE. Ah sure, that's the way! So what did yeh do, come home to see the auld match or what?

DANGER. What? Oh yeah. I came back to see the auld match. . . . Who's that?

MOLLY *is singing, 'Stranger in Paradise'.*

JOE. What? That's your auld flame Danger . . . Molly! Someone must have told her she had legs like a lark . . . Hey what do yeh think of this lad, Danger? Matty Whelan's son. That's Danger Doyle now boy and yeh dyin' to meet him.

DANGER. But sure he wouldn't remember me. He'd have only been a nipper when I went away.

JOE. He heard of yeh though, Danger. Hey Georgie, show him the jersey yeh got. He got a jersey a few weeks ago off of big Red O'Neill. Where is it Georgie?

GEORGIE. It's in the bag there.

JOE *takes the jersey out of the bag and holds it up.*

JOE. What do yeh make of that Danger? Feel the heft of it. You'd want to be Charles Atlas to lift it nearly. He'll be a fine fella when that fits him won't he? Of course these fellas think they're big lads goin' around here yeh know? They think they're the bees knees so they do. I mean I try to tell them the way it used to be with you and me but sure . . . We made fellas hop around here, me and him. Didn't we Danger? I was just tellin' Georgie the other day about all the times we used to break into this place and how they'd never have caught us at all if it hadn't 've been for the auld one who spotted that the writin' was out in front of the stamp. Jaysus we made some money out of it boy. How many times did we knock off this place Danger before they copped on?

DANGER. Twice.

JOE. What? Ah no it was more than that Danger.

DANGER. We broke in here twice. We made thirty bob each on the first transaction and they had a trap set for us the second time round. I climbed in through that big bay window there. You were outside keepin' nix. Or supposed

ACT ONE 27

to be keepin' nix I should say.

JOE. That's right, I had hurt me foot or somethin' hadn't I?

DANGER. Yeah. Anyway, the next thing I know I've set off some sort of an alarm and there was cops swarmin' all over me. No sign of your man here at all of course.

JOE. I whistled out to yeh Danger.

DANGER. Yes yeh did yeah. Yeh must have whistled under your breath then because I never heard yeh. I wouldn't mind but yeh could hear a pin drop in the place the same night. Suddenly anyway there's cops comin' in through every door and window in the shop and that big cop whatshisname is tryin' to grab a hold of me. Sanders.

JOE. Oh yeah, Big Sanders. He was a right bastard that fella was wasn't he?

DANGER. I took a swing at him and he downed me with a box in the jaw. I wasn't much of a hard case after that. Me knees just buckled from in under me I swear. Then he picked me up and shagged me into the back of the squad car like an auld sack of potatoes.

JOE. We all went up to the courtroom the next day, a whole crowd of us – do yeh remember Danger? I'll never forget that boy. Poor Danger gettin' led in with a great pair of handcuffs on him and he nearly cryin'. It was queer funny.

DANGER. What do yeh mean nearly cryin? I was cryin'. I'm goin' to tell yeh one thing but it's a good job I wasn't able to get at you that time because I'd 've kilt yeh.

JOE. I whistled out to yeh Danger.

DANGER *sighs, turns away chuckling.*

DANGER (*turning to* GEORGIE *with the jersey*). So when did he give yeh this then?

GEORGIE. After the Leinster final. He just tossed it out into the crowd and I caught it.

DANGER. He's a good hurler ain't he?

GEORGIE. Yeah.

JOE. He's the best, Danger . . . So what does it feel like to be home, boy?

DANGER. What do it feel like? . . . I'll tell yeh lads, today I found meself snakin' through the streets of me own hometown like a whatdoyoucallit . . . Ah I can't think of the word now.

JOE. A fugitive, Danger. Like a fugitive.

DANGER. Yeah. A fugitive.

MOLLY *enters*.

MOLLY. Are youse not gone yet? It'll be nearly time to come back before yeh leave at all.

JOE. What do yeh think of this fella Molly?

MOLLY. Who's that?

DANGER. How are yeh, honey bunch?

MOLLY. How are yeh? When did you get home?

DANGER. Yesterday mornin'.

MOLLY. Had yeh a good crossin'?

DANGER. Yeah it was alright. A bit bumpy at times like, yeh know but . . . it was alright.

MOLLY. I heard you were back alright but to tell you the truth I was hard set to believe it.

DANGER. Why's that?

JOE. Good man, Danger.

MOLLY. So how long are yeh stayin' for anyway?

DANGER. I don't know. A couple of days.

JOE. He came over to see the auld match, Molly. Hey Georgie, keep an eye out for that bus there will yeh?

JOE *goes out to the toilet*.

DANGER. So how are yeh keepin' anyway, Molly?

MOLLY. How do I look?

DANGER. You look grand.

MOLLY. Do I?

DANGER. Yeah . . . Were yeh surprised to see me?

MOLLY. Yeah I was. But then you were always full of

ACT ONE 29

surprises weren't yeh?

DANGER. Was I?

MOLLY. Give us a fag will yeh?

He gives her a cigarette and lights her up.

Jaysus look at me. I'm shakin' like a leaf here.

DANGER. Why?

MOLLY. Because I've just seen a ghost that's why.

DANGER. Is that what I am, a ghost?

MOLLY. Yeah, for want of a better word.

DANGER. Yeah well, don't worry about it hon. I didn't come back here to haunt you.

MOLLY. You didn't need to come back to do that Danger.

JOE (*returning*). Anythin' stirrin' Georgie?

GEORGIE. No.

JOE. Hah? Lord Jaysus ain't this awful ain't it!

He storms towards the front door.

I'll see yeh tomorrow night in Larkin's, Danger, as soon as we get back. That's if we ever get there in the first place of course. Where are yeh stoppin' anyway?

DANGER. The County Hotel.

JOE. Huh, swanky. I'll see yeh, Danger.

DANGER. Good luck Joe . . . He seems to be in right form anyway. I was often readin' about him in the local paper. He's into everythin' ain't he? Darts and football and what have yeh. Jaysus every time yeh turn a page there he is starin' up at yeh.

MOLLY. Yeah well Joe woke up one mornin' to find that there was a great big hole in his life yeh see. He's been tryin' to fill it up ever since . . . But sure I'll probably see yeh meself in Larkin's tomorrow night. I'll let yeh buy me a drink – for old time's sake.

She leaves. Silence.

DANGER. How is your Da, Georgie?

GEORGIE. Well, thanks. Sure, why don't yeh go on up to the house and see him?

DANGER. Ah no, I don't think so.

GEORGIE. Why not? I'd say he'd be delighted to see yeh.

Pause.

DANGER. Hey Georgie, have yeh any idea where Eileen is?

GEORGIE. She just slipped across to the pub for a minute to see her Da.

DANGER. Would yeh be able to go over and get her for me?

GEORGIE. But sure she'll be back in a minute.

DANGER. Yeah I know but I really don't want to hang around here too long like, yeh know.

GEORGIE *thinks about it. He acquiesces.*

DANGER. Good man Georgie. She's not goin' up to the match or anythin' is she?

GEORGIE. No.

JOE (*from the doorway*). Come on Georgie, we're bailin' out . . . The bus is here.

GEORGIE. Oh yeah, right. Any sign of Eileen?

JOE. She's on her way, come on. I told her you were here, Danger.

DANGER. Thanks Joe.

JOE. Come on Georgie, will yeh. There y'are now Danger, you'll have the run of the place to yourself. That's a right turn for the books alright ain't it? Come on Georgie.

JOE *leaves.*

GEORGIE (*stuffing the jersey back into his bag*). So how long are yeh goin' to hang around for anyway?

DANGER. I'm goin' back tomorrow evenin', Georgie, and I'm goin' to tell yeh one thing but it'll be a queer long time before you see me again boy . . . You'll be well after fillin' out that jersey by then so yeh will.

GEORGIE. We'll have a long wait for that I think.

DANGER. But sure what harm if yeh never fill it out Georgie. Aren't yeh big enough?

GEORGIE *exits.* **DANGER** *rambles around the shop, taking in his surroundings.* **EILEEN** *enters.*

How are yeh Eileen?

EILEEN. Hello.

DANGER. Do yeh know somethin', the smell out of this auld place brings back a queer lot of memories for me, I can tell yeh.

EILEEN. Does it? I didn't realise it had a smell of its own. What does it smell of anyway?

DANGER. Misfortune . . . How are yeh doin'?

EILEEN. Alright. Was that you who got me the locket from Carrington's, yeah?

DANGER. Yeah. Ah your Mammy asked me to get yeh somethin' for your birthday. I just thought I might as well get it over here, save me luggin' it all the way across. Was it alright for yeh after?

EILEEN. Yeah it was lovely. Thanks. Is me Mammy OK?

DANGER. Yeah. She's alright. She misses you terrible of course. She was wonderin' if maybe you'd come back with me – spend a bit of time with her.

EILEEN. Go back to London with yeh, yeh mean?

DANGER. Yeah. Just for a little while. Stay until Christmas maybe. What do yeh think?

EILEEN. I don't know.

DANGER. Well I mean to say you're not exactly over the moon about workin' here are yeh? Not accordin' to your letters anyway.

EILEEN. No, I'm not mad about the job but . . .

DANGER. Well there y'are then.

EILEEN. Is there no chance of me Mammy comin' over here?

DANGER. Naw, I don't think so, Eileen.

EILEEN *thinks about it and sighs.*

EILEEN. It's just that me Daddy might think that I was . . .

DANGER. What? Look if you're wantin' me to talk to him, just say so. I mean to say, Eileen, it's only for a couple of months.

Pause.

EILEEN. When are yeh goin' back anyway?

DANGER. Tomorrow evenin' . . . I have to be back at work be Monday night yeh see.

EILEEN (*angrily*). I just don't see why she can't come over here.

SPEAKER. Runners and riders at Kelso as in your morning papers. Non-runners at Newmarket, Number Seven, The Baker's Wife and Number Nine, Italian Lady. Number Seven and Number Nine, non-runners at Newmarket.

EILEEN *goes behind the counter to mark off the non-runners on the result sheet. Then she comes out to repeat the process on the sheet above the bench.* DANGER *watches her.*

DANGER. Your Ma don't like the idea of you workin' here at all, yeh know.

EILEEN (*sulkily*). Why's that?

DANGER. Ah, I don't know. I think she keeps imaginin' all the hard cases and chancers that are comin' in and out of here all the time.

EILEEN. Most of them are alright.

Pause as EILEEN *fiddles with the locket.*

DANGER. Your Mammy'd love to come back here Eileen – to see you, to see your little room and all. But let's face it, it's not as simple as that is it? Jaysus hon, around here they'd turn the poor crator to dust so they would . . . (*Pause.*) Yeh know I can still remember one of the very first presents your Mammy ever bought for you. It was a little sort of a music box. When yeh opened the lid a tune spilled out of it. We bought it in a shop in Shepherds Bush market. Heidelmann or somethin' was your man's name who owned the shop. He stamped his name on the cardboard box it came in. Jewish I think he was. 'Eileen'd

ACT ONE 33

love that now' your Mammy said when she saw it in the window, a great fancy design on it and all. Jaysus there was more wrappin' went on that present than little . . . What's up Eileen?

EILEEN *is weeping.*

EILEEN. I don't know. It's all so sudden. One minute I'm here, the next you want to just whisk me away. I'm not like you, yeh know. I can't just do things on the spur of the moment. I've me Daddy to think of.

DANGER. Yeah well I must confess I always was a spur of the moment man alright. Did yeh know I once climbed up to the top of Rowe Street chapel and hung me hat on the steeple. I just saw the ladders there, took a figeary and up I went. And another time we were all at this dance in the Town Hall and the County Manager's daughter was at it. I'm not coddin' yeh, nobody had the nerve to ask the girl up for a dance. So I just went over and asked her. She got up with me too . . . Your Mammy's terrible depressed, yeh know. She's on these auld tablets and all. I think if she saw you again she might be alright. Yeh should have come over to see her by now anyway Eileen . . .! She never stops talkin' about you, yeh know. I'm not coddin' yeh, she never stops. Eileen! Eileen! Eileen! – mornin', noon, and night.

Pause as EILEEN *looks into his sad eyes.*

EILEEN. Me Daddy 'll go mad . . .

EILEEN *goes and sits in the alcove of the bay window. Silence.*

DANGER (*moving closer to her*). Reinmann was his name though not Heidelmann. Reinmann – the fella that sold us the music box. He had a scutty shop in Shepherds Bush market. Bracelets and rings and that kind of thing. It had a galvanised roof. When it rained you could hardly hear your ears in the place. Some auld fella had slipped on a little rainbow of oil in the street that day. I picked him up and brought him into the shop, put him sittin' down on a chair. Your man made him a cup of tea. He was a nice enough fella – Reinmann. Stamped his name on nearly everythin' he sold. We were drenched that day goin' around in the rain, your Mammy and me. I had a great big hole in me shoe I remember, and your Mammy had one of those enormous headscarves wrapped around her.

She looked really pale. I got a bit of a fright when I caught a glimpse of her in a shop window – her pale face hidin' behind the rain. When we got back to the auld flat we were livin' in, I lit a fire and she sat hunched over it for hours on end starin' into the flames with the music box on her lap. I think that's when it began to dawn on me that there was a certain corner of her heart that I'd never be able to sweep clean.

Silence. DANGER *looks down to see* EILEEN *staring up at him, tears in her eyes.*

Do yeh fancy havin' your tea with me this evenin' down in the County Hotel?

EILEEN (*tearfully*). That'd be nice.

DANGER. A high tea on a low table hah?

EILEEN *looks into his eyes and smiles sadly.* DANGER *slowly rises and leaves.*

SPEAKER. The one fifteen at Newmarket. Royal York three-to-one. Splash seven-to-two. Time Out and The Tablemaker six-to-one. Tar and Feathered thirteen-to-two Daffy's Lad eight-to-one. Cool as a Breeze and Haymaker . . .

EILEEN *rises. She goes to the result sheet to mark up the horses. She breaks down and cries.*

Lights down.

ACT TWO

Scene One

The betting shop. EILEEN *is behind the counter working her way through a skewer of dockets. There is a suitcase standing close by.* MOLLY *enters.*

MOLLY. What's up Eileen?

EILEEN. Nothin'. I'm just finishin' off a bit of work, that's all.

MOLLY. Of a Sunday night! I thought there was someone after breakin' into the place or somethin'.

MOLLY *lights up a cigarette.*

EILEEN. Were yeh over in Larkin's Molly?

MOLLY. Yeah.

EILEEN. Is me Daddy over there?

MOLLY. Yes he is. He's in right form over there. There's a great stave altogether goin' on. Young Lugs McGuire has the guitar out and everythin'. I had three or four drinks meself this evenin'. I don't know who was buyin' 'em nor nothin'. I drank 'em anyway Eileen. To hell with the lot of them. If we had lost the match today we would have had to listen to them all moanin' for the next fortnight.

EILEEN. Is Georgie there?

MOLLY. That's what I was just goin' to say to yeh. Georgie Whelan sang, 'One Way Love' over there tonight and I swear to God Eileen it was only beautiful. They tore the place down for him so they did. And then Lugs McGuire sang the song that he made up about Red O'Neill. Ah yeh should hear it. It's great. He's after addin' another verse to it about all the lads who were on the bus goin' up to the match. Your Da and everyone is mentioned. Little Mickey Morris is doin' his nut because it kind of insinuates that himself and Big Mag Delaney 'll be gettin' engaged shortly. And Joe! – ah be Jaysus Joe bet the bun altogether. He sang 'I gave my wedding dress away', which he dedicated to Big Mag who of course was engaged about three times before. Joe said that she ruptured the first two fellas and the third lad got sense.

MOLLY *laughs*. EILEEN *is unmoved*. MOLLY *spies the suitcase*.

Well what did yeh think of the other fella comin' home?

EILEEN. Who's that?

MOLLY. Danger Doyle! Ah now Eileen, don't try and tell me that yeh never knew he was back.

EILEEN. Oh I knew he was back alright.

MOLLY. By Jaysus he has some neck on him though Eileen hasn't he? As brazen as yeh please, he comes waltzin' into the street yesterday, a great suit and tie and him and all. I thought it was Montgomery Clift or someone for a minute. 'How are yeh honey bunch?', says he to me, a fancy twang in his voice. He's stoppin' down in the County Hotel I believe. I suppose none of his own would have him. He was supposed to come into Larkin's for a few drinks this evenin' but he never showed up. He must have had more important things to do I suppose . . . So what are yeh goin' to do Eileen?

EILEEN. I don't know.

MOLLY. I'd stay well clear of him if I were you hon. Take it from one who knows and let him go back to where he came from because he's trouble with a capital T that fella is. Yes, a capital T.

EILEEN. Do yeh not think he's changed Molly?

MOLLY. Changed? People don't change Eileen. Not really. Underneath they stay the same . . . Yeh know sometimes you really remind me of your Mammy. The way yeh looked at me that time now – so secretive or somethin'. I don't know what it was about her but she always seemed to know somethin' that we didn't. Some little thing that set her apart from the rest of us. Somethin' so simple that it must have been starin' me right in the face, only I could never for the life of me figure out what it was. I wouldn't mind but I always felt that if I had been able to crack it I could have been somebody in this town. But I never did. I never found out what it was that set her apart. You're lucky Eileen. I was often watchin' yeh walkin' down the street. Or comin' out of Byrne's Café with Johnny Doran or someone. You get that confidence from your Mammy. I've only felt like that once in me life. It was a few years ago now. I took a good look in the mirror and I was surprised to find that I liked what I saw there. So I primped meself up and went to pay a call on this lonely man I know – because let's face it if a woman can't help to mend a broken heart then what the hell's the point of it all. Well, his face dropped when he opened the door and saw me standin' there. I told him out straight what I had come for. 'Go Away' he said and he shut the door in me face. (*She laughs.*) Huh, some of us have it is right! I bet nobody 'll ever shut a door in your face, Eileen.

MOLLY *looks blatantly down at the suitcase and then back at* EILEEN.

You're worse Eileen, havin' anything to do with him.

EILEEN. Ah he's alright. I'm sure he's not the worst of them.

MOLLY. Look Eileen, you don't know him. I know him. I know all belongin' to him. He never worked a day in his life. He wouldn't work in a fit. I'm tellin' yeh you're better off stayin' well away from him altogether. Anyway ain't yeh grand and snug where yeh are, with your own little room and your records and all without gettin' involved with the likes of him.

STEVEN *enters*.

EILEEN. Hello Daddy.

STEVEN. Eileen.

MOLLY. Steven there 'll vouch for that now . . . Georgie Whelan singin' 'One Way Love'. Beautiful Steven, wasn't it?

STEVEN. Yeah.

MOLLY. He has a grand voice, hasn't he?

STEVEN. Yeah. He's a nice singer alright.

MOLLY. I was just tellin' Eileen about it here. And did yeh

hear the song Lugs McGuire made up? What was the part in it about you Steven?

EILEEN. Did you get anythin' to eat today Daddy?

STEVEN. Yeah I had a bowl of soup and a few sandwiches earlier on.

MOLLY. Steven Redmond let out a roar or somethin' wasn't it?

EILEEN (*going behind the partition*). Huh, you'll get fat on that.

MOLLY. No. Steven Redmond let out a shout though.

STEVEN. What's goin' on Eileen?

MOLLY (*sings*).
  Steven Redmond let out a shout
  Oh says he there is no doubt . . .

EILEEN. I'll tell yeh after Daddy.

MOLLY (*sings*).
  That Red O'Neill is . . .

But sure I don't suppose you ever found out what it was that set her apart either Steven did yeh?

STEVEN. What?

JOE *and* GEORGIE *enter, arms around each other and singing. They are wearing team sashes and hats and scarves etc.*

JOE and GEORGIE (*sing*).
  Oh the Wayward Wind is a restless wind
  A restless wind that yearns to wander
  And I was born the next of kin
  The next of kin to the Wayward Wind.

MOLLY *joins in with the singing. She waltzes around the place, dancing over to* STEVEN *and forcing him to dance with her.* EILEEN *emerges to see her father abruptly breaking away from* MOLLY's *grasp.*

MOLLY. What's wrong with yeh Steven? Jaysus you're as miserable. No wonder your missus ran off on yeh.

MOLLY *goes and joins* GEORGIE *and* JOE *in song. She takes the scarf from* GEORGIE *and drapes it around her own neck.*

ACT TWO 39

GEORGIE, JOE *and* MOLLY (*sing*).
>In a lonely shack by a railroad track
>I spent my younger days
>And I guess the sound of the outward bound
>Made me a slave to my wandering ways.

JOE breaks away while the others keep singing.

JOE. Well Steven, what did yeh think of that then?

STEVEN. What's that?

JOE. Today! What did yeh think of it?

STEVEN. God, it was a right day.

JOE (*passionately*). Yeah but what did yeh think of it though? Did we do it or not? Yes or no?

STEVEN. Ah we did it alright.

JOE. Hah? Put it there me auld flower, we hurled 'em out of it so we did. Did yeh ever in all your born days Steven see anythin' like that last goal that Big Red O'Neill scored. Be the Lord Harry tonight, he buried it into the back of the net and that's all's about it.

GEORGIE. A beautiful goal.

JOE. What?

GEORGIE. It was a beautiful goal and I don't care what anyone says about it.

JOE. Beautiful! I'm goin' to tell yeh one thing here and now for nothin' boy but that was a classic goal so it was. They'll be debatin' and discussin' that goal for a queer long time to come you mark my words. Am I right or am I wrong Steven?

STEVEN *nods.*

GEORGIE. It was a deadly goal alright, no doubt about it.

JOE. Deadly! Meself and Mickey Morris kissed and hugged one another so hard that people started wonderin' about us, that's how deadly it was. Yes, you're livin' in the greatest little town in Ireland so yeh are boy and yeh don't even realise it. Put it there Steven, we hurled 'em out of it, so we did.

They shake hands. JOE *spies* MOLLY *eyeing them scornfully.*

Hey Steven, what would yeh think of a one who wouldn't even cheer for her own home town on the day of the All Ireland Final? What would yeh do with her eh . . .? Wouldn't even support her own flesh and blood. I don't know. Ah sure, what harm. We did it without her anyway.

GEORGIE *yelps*.

MOLLY. What do yeh mean 'we'? I didn't hear your name gettin' called out on the television or anythin'.

JOE. What did yeh say?

MOLLY. You heard me.

JOE. I didn't hear yeh. What did yeh say?

MOLLY. How many goals did you score today . . . How many balls did Georgie there put over the bar? The way you're talkin' anyone 'd think that you had somethin' to do with Big Red's goal. You had nothin' to do with it boy. Big Red O'Neill scored the goal all by himself.

JOE. I was there to cheer him on anyway. More than you were.

MOLLY. You had nothin' to do with it.

STEVEN. That's where you're wrong girl.

JOE. What do yeh mean I had nothin' to do with it?

STEVEN. No one man can . . .

JOE. I'm a Wexfordman and he's a Wexfordman.

MOLLY. So?

STEVEN. . . . achieve what a whole team can achieve. No one individual can . . .

JOE. So it's the same thing. When he scores I score. Or we score I should say.

MOLLY. Ah will yeh go away out of that and don't be annoyin' yourself Joe.

STEVEN. . . . even hope to whatdoyoucallit . . .

JOE. I wouldn't expect you to understand Molly.

STEVEN. I've been goin' to hurlin' matches for a queer long time now and if there's one thing that I've . . .

JOE. It's beyond your comprehension girl. You're worse than Steven.

STEVEN. What?

JOE. Sure that one wouldn't know her arse from her elbow now regardin' hurlin'.

MOLLY. I know as much as you about it I'd say.

JOE. Yes yeh do yeah. Look Molly yeh might as well admit it, yeh don't know the first thing about it.

MOLLY. Yeah well, maybe I don't know a whole lot about it but I'll tell yeh one thing I do know though. Big Red O'Neill must be browned off carryin' you crowd of ejits on his back everywhere he goes. It's a wonder some of yeh wouldn't get down and walk a bit of the way once in a while.

JOE. Hey, there's no man ever had to carry me on his back nor ever will either. No one had to carry me into Croke Park this afternoon. I walked in there of me own free will. (MOLLY *scoffs*.) Yeh see the trouble with you Molly is yeh have no time for this town. Well I have because I happen to believe that a man without a hometown is nothin'. Am I right or am I wrong Steven?

STEVEN. That's right. A man without a hometown is nothin'. He's lost.

JOE. Now yeh said it Steven. Lost is right. In the wilderness he is.

MOLLY. Are you two gone soft in the head or what? I mean what's this town ever done for any of you, only laughed at yez.

JOE. Hey, this town, nor nobody in it for that matter, has ever laughed at me mate.

MOLLY. They laughed at yeh. And do yeh want to know why?

JOE. No one in this town has ever laughed at me.

MOLLY. Well I'll tell yeh why. Because for the past ten years you've been like an auld chicken without a head runnin' around the place – organisin' this and organisin' that.

JOE. I wasn't the only one that Danger left behind Molly.

MOLLY. No but you're the one who does most of the bullshittin' about him every chance yeh get. (*Pause*.) Huh, next you'll be tryin' to tell me that nobody has ever laughed at Steven there either.

STEVEN. I'll have you know that I've never done anythin' in this town to be ashamed of.

MOLLY. Yeh must have a queer bad memory then Steven.

STEVEN. What do yeh mean?

MOLLY. Your name was scrawled all over half the walls of the town man. *Steven Redmond is a eunuch*. Do yeh not remember that one Steven? Well I do. And *Ole King Cole lives in a brothel*. Georgie did that one. Yeah, good old Georgie.

JOE. You're out of order now Molly.

MOLLY. Who the hell do you think yeh are anyway Steven, goin' around shuttin' doors in people's faces and walkin' around with your nose in the air. Jaysus Christ man anyone'd think that you had . . .

JOE. You're way out of order girl.

MOLLY. Ah go and fuck off Joe will yeh.

MOLLY *retreats to a corner*.

STEVEN. I don't see why I have to stand here in me own hometown and listen to this kind of talk. I mean to say I've never done anything to be . . .

STEVEN *sees the suitcase for the first time. He looks from it to* EILEEN. *Stunned, he looks around him at the others like a bereaved man and then he goes and sits at the table in the anteroom.*

EILEEN (*furious, going to* MOLLY). There was no need to rear up on him like that.

MOLLY. Yes there was. I'm sick and tired of him lookin' down his nose at me.

EILEEN. What do yeh mean?

MOLLY. He looks down his nose at me all the time, turnin' away when he meets me in the street and all. Jaysus, he wouldn't even give us a feckin' auld dance at the factory reunion last year.

EILEEN. So what? He ought to kiss your feet every time he meets yeh now.

MOLLY. Look Eileen, you're not the one who feels like a piece of dirt every time he turns to look at yeh. Anyone 'd think I had done somethin' on him. It's not my fault that your Ma cleared off to England. If he had 've been man enough in the first place to hang on to her he wouldn't be in this predicament now.

EILEEN. You're only takin' it out on him because Danger is back in town and because he came back for me and not for you.

MOLLY. That has nothin' to do with it. I wouldn't touch Danger Doyle nor anythin' belongin' to him now with a forty foot pole.

EILEEN. Oh yeah, pull the other one Molly. You laugh about me Daddy's name appearin' on half the walls of the town but if the truth be told you'd have given your right arm once upon a time for your name to be up there too. Danger and Molly in the middle of a great big heart or somethin'. And now yeh have the nerve to make out that Danger was never anything but a dirty corner boy and yeh talk about me Mammy as if she was just another little workin' class bitch in heat. Well you'd want to take a good look at your own poxy life Molly before yeh go tearin' strips off of other people's.

EILEEN *walks away, down the steps and across to the counter.*

GEORGIE. Well said Eileen. By Jaysus you're well able to fight your corner alright. Ain't she Joe?

JOE. What?

GEORGIE. I say she's well able to stand up for herself.

EILEEN *throws him a contemptuous look.* JOE *hushes him up.* GEORGIE *goes to* EILEEN.

Yeh know somethin' Eileen, this has certainly been an enlightenin' few days alright hasn't it? – between one thing and another.

EILEEN. What do yeh mean?

GEORGIE. Well I mean to say you found out somethin' about me and I found out somethin' about you . . .

EILEEN. You found out somethin' about me? What? What was it?

GEORGIE. Ain't that right Joe?

JOE. What?

GEORGIE. I say we found out a lot about ourselves in the past few days.

JOE. Feckin' right we did. We hurled 'em out of it that's all.

EILEEN. Georgie, what did you find out about me?

GEORGIE. What?

EILEEN. What did yeh find out about me?

GEORGIE. Let's just say that I happened to overhear someone mention that famous afternoon you and the carnival boy spent in your house while your Da was away at a match somewhere.

EILEEN. What about it?

GEORGIE. How the pair of yeh slipped off hand in hand down to the bedroom when no one was lookin'.

EILEEN. Yeah well it wasn't quite like that Georgie.

GEORGIE. Oh yeah. And what was it quite like then?

EILEEN. Ah it doesn't matter now.

GEORGIE. Yes it does matter. It matters to me anyway. I've known you for as long as I can remember and in all that time I've never even tried to . . .

EILEEN. What?

GEORGIE. You must have had a right laugh about me did yeh – you and him?

EILEEN. Georgie I've never laughed at you in me life. I've laughed with yeh and about yeh but I've never laughed at yeh.

GEORGIE. Yeh must have. I mean while I was hangin' around here all the time, gettin' sweet nothin' off of you, you were . . .

EILEEN. I was what? Look Georgie, it was never supposed to be like that between you and me.

GEORGIE. Yeah well let's face it, you weren't exactly what you were lettin' on to be were yeh?

EILEEN *throws her eyes to heaven.*

I don't like anyone tryin' to gull me Eileen.

EILEEN. Sure God help yeh, you're killed aren't yeh? Jaysus, and I thought I could depend on you.

GEORGIE. Yeah well, that was before I found out what you were made of wasn't it? That was before I found out that you were just like your Ma – a real skeet goin' around.

EILEEN. What are yeh tryin' to do boy, scorch the ground from in under us or somethin'?

GEORGIE. You're the one who's done the scorchin' Eileen, not me. For the past few days my heart's been down in my shoes or somewhere over you girl . . . Yeh keep me hangin' on all the time Eileen so that I don't know whether I'm comin' or goin' with yeh. I mean I don't know what I'm supposed to do. What am I supposed to do?

EILEEN. I'm sorry, Georgie. I didn't know yeh felt like that. It was never supposed to be like that between you and me.

GEORGIE. Ah forget about it. I don't think you'll be seein' a whole lot of me around here any more anyway. I wouldn't lower meself to tell yeh nothin' but the truth.

GEORGIE *turns away from her.* EILEEN *is saddened. She reaches under the counter and takes the record out. She leaves it on the counter in front of him and she goes off to the office.* GEORGIE *turns to watch her go. He picks up the record and begins to smash it off of the edge of the counter.*

JOE. What's the matter Georgie? What's up?

GEORGIE. Hey Joe, remember what you were sayin' the other day about Eileen.

JOE. What?

GEORGIE. Eileen!

JOE. What about her?

GEORGIE. Remember what you were sayin' about her?

MOLLY. What ails him?

JOE. He's alright. A bit too much to drink that's all. He'll be alright.

GEORGIE (*gripping* JOE). Listen to me Joe, will yeh. This is important.

JOE. What's wrong with yeh?

GEORGIE. I need to know if what you were sayin' about Eileen the other day is . . .

JOE. Forget about Eileen, Georgie will yeh.

GEORGIE. What?

JOE. Forget about her.

> JOE *frees himself from* GEORGIE's *grip and breaks away.* GEORGIE *plonks himself down on the bench.*

Young fellas!

> JOE *goes up into the anteroom. He takes a naggon of whisky from his coat pocket.*

Do you want a drop of whisky Steven?

> STEVEN *shakes his head.* JOE *goes in behind the counter and down into the office. He returns with two cups and he begins to pour out some whisky. He hands one of the cups to* MOLLY. *He takes a slug himself and then he holds his cup aloft and sings.*

JOE (*sings*).
> I want to be your lover.
> But your friend is all I stay
> You leave me halfway to Paradise
> So near, yet so far away.

Do you remember that one Molly? You, me and Danger down in Byrne's Café, knockin' back the Coca Cola, me and Danger dressed up to kill in a couple of suits we just bought on the never never. Yeh know I was often thinkin' Molly that if Danger hadn't come along when he did you and me would've nearly . . .

MOLLY. What? You and me would've never nearly nothin'. Sure you were never any good with women.

JOE. Hey, I knew me onions when it came to women mate.

MOLLY. Yeh never had any way with women.

JOE. And what about June Carty? And young Whitney? Or Big Mag Delaney? Or that young one used to live on the corner of King street there. The litany of women goes on and on I don't mind tellin' yeh. And when I'd get on the little football table the whole place'd flock around me because I was a bit of a shark at that game. You ask Danger. Even he used to bow to me boy.

MOLLY. Pocket billiards 'd be more like it I'd say.

JOE. And what about those two English girls who came home here one summer. One of them was dyin' alive about me.

MOLLY. Yeah and you spent the whole summer threatenin' to ask her to go to the pictures with yeh, so that in the end Mickey Morris asked her out and that was that.

JOE. I asked her out.

MOLLY. Yes yeh did, yeah!

GEORGIE *begins to cough and splutter as he makes for the door.*

JOE. Good man Georgie. Get it up out of yeh me auld son.

JOE *looks at* GEORGIE *and laughs. He pours some more whisky into* MOLLY's *cup and toasts.*

JOE. Anyway Molly, here's to Red O'Neill and the sportin' life.

MOLLY. What the hell would you know about the sportin' life? A hurler on the ditch is all you ever were.

JOE. And what's wrong with that? Someone has to stand on the sidelines and keep the auld thing goin' yeh know. We all can't be Red O'Neill's or anythin' . . . Lose yourself in the crowd Molly, that's my motto.

MOLLY. Yeah I know. But then you're probably hidin' from the fact that yeh once turned your back on your best friend just when he needed yeh the most. And then yeh had the nerve to laugh at him when he cried.

JOE (*sadly*). Only out of relief Molly because he didn't give me away . . . He didn't give me away.

MOLLY. Yeah well, don't worry about it Joe. He made up for it in the end. He betrayed the whole shaggin' lot of us.

JOE. No, you're wrong there Molly. Danger Doyle never betrayed no one in this town.

MOLLY. Ah.

GEORGIE *returns*.

JOE. I'm goin' to tell yeh one thing Molly here and now for nothin' because it's high time that this whole thing was whatdoyoucallit . . .

MOLLY. You're drunk.

JOE. What?

MOLLY. Go away from me will yeh.

JOE. I'm not drunk. Listen to me. I was Danger's best mate and I didn't even know he was goin' to run away. I was drinkin' with him the night before he went and he didn't even tell me. And I was his best mate. But he didn't betray me. Yeh can't say that he betrayed me.

GEORGIE. Hey Joe, he's no use boy. He's no friggin' use.

MOLLY. Now yeh said it Georgie. He's no use is right. He's a dead bloody loss so he is. And then he comes home and you fellas roll out the red carpet for him. I'd like me job now.

GEORGIE. There's no welcome on my mat for him anyway, Molly. Nor for anyone belongin' to him either.

JOE. Ah that's a load of balls Georgie.

GEORGIE. There's no need to stand up for him all the time Joe.

JOE. I'm not standin' up for him Georgie. I'm just sayin' that's all.

Pause.

MOLLY. Yes, I'd like me job.

Pause.

JOE. There's a thing I was just thinkin' of today though Molly. About the time Danger got that job workin' on the bumpers above in that auld fairground remember? And he used to let you and me go on 'em for nothin' all the time. My jeans were so tight that I nearly did meself a mischief one night climbin' down off the merry-go-round. Oh the pain of it! 'Sealed with a Kiss', blarin' out over the big loudspeakers.

(*Sings.*) Oh it's gonna be a long lonely summer . . .
By Jaysus it very nearly was too.

Pause.

MOLLY. You always played sad songs on the jukebox.

A wild cheer outside and a host of voices singing, 'One Way Love', to a simple guitar accompaniment.

JOE. There's your auld song now, Georgie.

JOE *goes to the door.*

GEORGIE. What can yeh do with a girl like that Joe eh? I mean what are yeh supposed to do with her?

JOE. Forget about her Georgie. Because yeh might as well be pissin' against the wind as to wish for somethin' yeh can't have. Am I right or am I wrong Molly?

MOLLY. Some people are born to be hurt, some to do the hurtin'. It's as simple as that. That's just the nature of things.

JOE. Come on and we'll all go out around the auld bonfire and have a bit of a singsong Molly. Come on. Are yeh comin' out Georgie?

GEORGIE. Naw.

JOE. Come on out of that.

JOE *leaves just as* EILEEN *comes out of the office.* GEORGIE *looks at her and then guiltily turns away.* MOLLY *is sitting in the alcove of the bay window.* EILEEN *looks out through the little window behind the counter.*

VOICES (*singing*).
  While you're up there and I'm sinking fast
  You must be living in a plastercast
  I don't think I'm gonna last my whole life through
  With you . . .

DANGER DOYLE *enters.*

VOICES (*singing*).
  One way love.
  One way love.

The song ends and a great cheer goes up around the bonfire.

DANGER. How are yeh Eileen?

EILEEN. Hello.

DANGER. Is that your case? (EILEEN *nods.*) There's a taxi waitin' across the street to take us down to the harbour.

Pause.

EILEEN. I'll get me coat.

She goes down to the office. Silence as DANGER *looks from* MOLLY *to* GEORGIE *to* STEVEN. *A wild cheer outside.*

DANGER. I'd say there was a good auld atmosphere up at the match today Molly was there?

MOLLY. I don't know. I wasn't at it meself. You'd want to ask Steven about that . . . Anyway I didn't think you'd have any interest in it one way or another.

DANGER. Ah yeah. I was watchin' it on the box down in the hotel this afternoon. The camera panned in on the crowd there at one stage. I thought sure we'd catch a glimpse of one of the boys – Mickey Morris or someone.

MOLLY. But sure they're all outside now standing around the bonfire if you're wantin' to go and shake hands with any of them . . . (DANGER *shrugs.*) Go and climb down off of your high horse there mister. Who the hell do yeh think yeh are anyway?

DANGER. To tell yeh the truth Molly I'm half afraid to climb down in case I end up like your man whatshisname . . . Oisín. Do yeh remember that story? He came back from a place called Tír Na Nóg and as soon as he touched the ground he turned into an auld fella. I'll never forget the first mornin' the Christian Brother told us about that and I remember thinkin' at the time that a man'd want to be a bit soft in the head or somethin' to come back from a land of eternal youth just because he wanted to see his auld mates again. . . He must have had somethin' else on his mind Molly, hah?

MOLLY. Yeah.

JOE (*enters, laughing hysterically*). Little Mickey Morris is after gettin' so sick out there that he nearly put out the fire . . .

Hey Georgie, come on they're wantin' you to sing a song out here ... Oh be Jaysus look at Danger where he is. Hey, this one was blackguardin' the lot of us here today Danger.

DANGER. Among yeh be it, Joe.

JOE. What?

MOLLY. He said he don't want any part in the discussion. And who could blame the man. Anyone who runs away with a circus is hardly goin' to come back to see an auld sideshow now is he?

JOE. Did yeh go up to the match after Danger?

DANGER. No.

JOE. That's a pity. You should have come up on the bus with us. Yeh could have had your name mentioned in young Lugs McGuire's song now.

MOLLY. That man has no desire to be swallowed up by the crowd like you yeh know Joe. He wants a song all to himself. Don't yeh Danger?

JOE. It wouldn't be the first time meself and Danger had songs written about us.

DANGER. Yeah but I think we made most of them up ourselves though Joe.

JOE. So what have yeh been up to since yeh got back?

DANGER. Ah I don't know. Just takin' a good look round really.

MOLLY. What, from your hotel window yeh mean?

DANGER. I went into Byrne's Café today.

MOLLY (*testily*). What for?

DANGER *shrugs*.

DANGER. I see the auld jukebox is still goin' strong down there anyway.

JOE. Yeah, still pumpin' away down there. I'm goin' to tell yeh one thing boy but they don't make 'em like that no more. So what did yeh think of the place? Still the same ain't it? Nothin' changes boy ... Jaysus we had some good times together though Danger, didn't we? Remember the day yeh cut the arse off of yourself gettin' out over the nun's wall. And the time yeh climbed up to the top of the chapel to hang your hat on the steeple. I'm not coddin' yeh boy but yeh nearly put the heart crossways in me that day lookin' at yeh. I must have had half your obituary written before yeh came back down . . . So what are yeh at over there this weather anyway Danger?

DANGER. I'm workin' in a car factory. Auld shift work.

JOE. I thought you were still with the cigarette people.

DANGER. No. I got sacked out of there for being overweight one night . . . five or six cartons overweight.

DANGER *grins.* JOE *thinks about it and laughs.*

JOE. Still the same auld Danger . . . Hey do yeh know who I bumped into the other day? That country girl that you walked home from a dance one night. Remember yeh walked about seven miles out into the country with her and she didn't even give yeh a good night kiss.

DANGER. I walked seven miles. Joe, you were the one who walked her home not me.

JOE. Ah come on now Danger, don't try and turn the tables on me. I remember you talkin' about the blisters on your feet the next day.

DANGER. The blisters on your feet yeh mean.

MOLLY. Oh for God's sake. Look if you two are goin' to kiss the past's arse all night long then I wish the pair of yeh would go somewhere else and do it.

JOE. What's wrong with you?

MOLLY. Yeh haven't seen each other in nearly ten years! Don't yeh have nothin' important to say to one another? Isn't there anythin' to forgive? Isn't there somethin' to forget?

JOE. The only thing meself and Danger have to say to one another is that we had some good times together. There's nothin' to either forgive or to forget. Ain't that right Danger?

DANGER. That's right Joe. Nothin' that time hasn't washed

ACT TWO 53

away by now anyway Molly.

MOLLY. Want to bet.

JOE. Ordinarily he means Molly. With ordinary people.

MOLLY. What's that supposed to mean?

JOE. It's a joke.

MOLLY. Oh stop. Sure you're a real Groucho Marx goin' around with your jokes.

She turns away. Pause.

JOE. We must take a bit of a stroll together around some of the auld haunts one day Danger, now that you're here. I'm goin' to tell yeh one thing boy but you won't believe some of the changes that are after . . .

EILEEN *enters, a small overnight case in her hand, her overcoat on.* DANGER's *gaze wanders towards her, stopping* JOE *in his tracks. All eyes are on* EILEEN *now.*

MOLLY (*toasting*). Welcome to the ranks of the left behind Georgie.

JOE. Are yeh off Danger?

DANGER *nods.*

I thought yeh were hangin' around for a while?

DANGER. I have to get back to work Joe like, yeh know.

JOE *indicates that he understands. He goes to* DANGER.

JOE. Well put it there me auld stock. (*They shake hands.*) And don't leave it so long the next time will yeh? Because before yeh know it they'll be plantin' one or the other of us in the ground so they will.

DANGER. Yeah, see yeh Joe.

JOE. And another thing, we broke into this place more than twice. It was five or six times at the very least and I won't have you sayin' anythin' to the contrary boy . . . And listen, I did whistle out to yeh that night, Danger. I know you said yeh never heard me and all but I whistled out to yeh. I swear.

Silence as the two men stare into each other's eyes. Then JOE *breaks away, winks and leaves.* DANGER *watches the empty doorway.* MOLLY *approaches.*

MOLLY. And I called out your name that day up in the courtroom when I saw yeh standin' there with the tears in your eyes.

DANGER. I never heard yeh.

MOLLY. That's because it was kind of soft and low, Danger.

GEORGIE *laughs.*

What's so funny?

GEORGIE. Danger Doyle, the big hard man cryin' his eyes out up in the courtroom.

GEORGIE *rises and laughing manically he stumbles across to* DANGER.

Cryin' his eyes out up in the courtroom he was. Danger Doyle, the big hard man.

GEORGIE *leaves shouting at the top of his voice all over the street.* EILEEN, *concerned goes to look out the little window.*

The big famous Danger Doyle cryin' like a baby up in the courtroom ... (*He laughs manically.*)

DANGER. That's it Georgie boy, you shout it from the rooftops son.

MOLLY. What did you want to come back here for anyway? As if I wasn't tangled up enough already without havin' to see you again.

DANGER. I just came back to kiss the cross they hung me on Molly. Or maybe I came back to set you free.

MOLLY. Free? To do what? To go where?

Slight pause.

DANGER. To stay here?

MOLLY. Oh and I suppose we're all expected to be eternally grateful to the great Danger Doyle for settin' us free are we? Well let me tell you one thing Mister, here and now for nothin', but I don't need you nor any other fella like yeh either to set me free. I don't need you to ...

It is the calmness and tenderness in DANGER's *eyes that stops her from going on. She backs away to gaze lovingly at his face. Pause.*

Aw Danger . . . Doyle if you only knew! Yeh know when you ran away with her like that I kept tellin' meself that it wouldn't last, that it wouldn't be long until yeh came back again to me. I'd picture yeh strollin' into town, kickin' up the leaves, your hair fallin' down into your eyes the way it used to and I'd be smilin' away to meself at the very idea of it – in spite of the fact that there was a great big knot screwin' and twistin' inside of me all the time. After a while of course it all turned kind of sour so that in the end, I'm not coddin' yeh, I felt like some poor beast that had been left out too long in the rain. Yeh'd forgotten me yeh see. Yeh'd forgotten all about me.

DANGER. No Molly, I never forgot yeh hon. Never. Yeh know you were the first girl ever to make me feel half decent in this town and I'll always remember yeh for it. But that was a long time ago Molly and you can search me if yeh want but I swear to God I don't have what you seem to think I took from yeh.

Silence.

MOLLY. What am I goin' to do Danger?

He has no answer. Pause.

I'll see yeh.

DANGER. Yeah . . . see yeh Molly.

MOLLY *leaves.*

EILEEN. I've never seen Georgie like this before. Maybe I should go out to him.

DANGER. Leave him alone Eileen. He'll be alright. Who knows with a bit of luck he might wind up washin' my name away for once and for all . . . Are you alright?

EILEEN *nods. Pause.* DANGER *turns to* STEVEN.

I'm terrible sorry about the way things turned out Steven. I never meant to . . . Well I'm sorry about the way things went.

EILEEN. Danger says that me Mammy misses me terrible Daddy and that she's dyin' to see me again. I'm goin' to go back with him for a little while.

DANGER. She's a bit down in herself at the moment over there, Steven like, yeh know. I just felt that it might do her good to see Eileen again.

EILEEN. It's just for a while Daddy.

Pause.

STEVEN. And I thought I was goin' to sneak through life unnoticed . . . This town'll be the death of me yet.

STEVEN *rises and goes across to look out of the bay window.*

God I hate to see anybody carryin' a suitcase – anyone belongin' to me anyway. Would yeh believe it Eileen but I've never packed a bag in me life. Just sleepin' in Dublin last night now nearly put years on me. I can't understand why people can't stay put. I mean what's the attraction out there anyway? Everyone keeps reachin' for the moon. I wouldn't mind but half of them wouldn't even know what to do with it if it fell into their laps. It seems to be a mortal sin these days to want to stay where yeh are . . . Your Mammy was the very same. She was always wonderin' what was over the next hill. She was always wonderin' about somethin'. Jukebox fellas and carnival boys seemed to fascinate her. A fancy scarf blowin' in the wind, a tattoo, anythin' the least bit outlandish at all and she was off. I never knew whether I was comin' or goin' with her. I never really knew what way I was fixed with her at all to tell yeh the truth.

Pause.

EILEEN. I have to go to her Daddy. I mean if she's not goin' to come to me then I have to go to her don't I?

STEVEN *plonks himself down sadly into the alcove of the bay window. Outside the crowd are singing 'The Girl Of My Best Friend'.*

VOICES (*singing.*)
    The way she walks
    The way she talks
    How long can I pretend . . .

EILEEN. Don't I Daddy?

STEVEN *sighs and then nods in agreement. Pause.*

DANGER. I'll stick this out in the boot of the car Eileen.

DANGER *takes the suitcase and heads towards the door. He stops in the doorway.*

She's still terrible fond of you, yeh know Steven. She'd never let anyone say nothin' against yeh now nor nothin'.

Pause. DANGER *leaves. Silence except for the singing outside.*

STEVEN. I never meant to hinder yeh from seein' your Mammy or anythin' Eileen yeh know. Nor her from seein' you for that matter . . . It seems she more or less regarded me as some sort of an auld snare that she was all caught up in so while she had the chance she was goin' to make a run for it. In a taxi down to the harbour with Danger Doyle! It was all in the note that I found on top of me lunch box that mornin' – in her little dainty handwritin' . . . It broke my heart when she ran off on me like that yeh know. It broke me bloody heart so it did.

STEVEN *hangs his head sadly.* EILEEN *stands motionless, her eyes brimming with tears.* STEVEN *rises and braces himself.*

Are yeh alright for money?

EILEEN. Yeah, I've enough money . . . I'll write to yeh as soon as I get there.

STEVEN. Aye, do.

EILEEN *goes to him. They embrace.*

EILEEN. Goodbye Daddy.

EILEEN *breaks away. She takes a bunch of keys from her pocket and leaves them on the counter. She leaves.*

VOICES (*outside, singing*). Will My Aching Heart never mend . . .

STEVEN *goes across to the counter, picks up the keys and rattles them. He puts them in his pocket and then he goes in behind the counter to switch off the small light behind the partition. He comes out to the front door and lets off the catch on the lock. He switches out the main lights and leaves, closing the door behind him.*

VOICES (*outside, singing*).
   Oh will I always be in love
   With the girl of my best friend . . .

Lights down.

Ends.